This MAMMOTH belongs to

_____

_____

_____

SUN SNOW STARS SKY

Catherine and Laurence Anholt

MAMMOTH

Early in the morning the sun comes up.

Look out of your window. Is it...

frosty,

foggy,

wet,

windy,

hot,

hailing,

stormy,

snowing?

What's the weather like today?

On HOT days...

bees buzz,

tired dogs search for shade,

ice tastes nice.

Plants need a drink too.

We don't wear many clothes,

and everyone likes to be outdoors.

What do you do on HOT days?

Do you watch the clouds sail by
in all shapes and sizes?

What else do you see in the sky?

On COLD days...

puddles turn
to ice,

cars are hard
to start.

We have
warm drinks,

and wear
lots of clothes.

We can see our breath in the air.

We might find footprints in the snow.

What do you do on COLD days?

Some animals sleep all winter
and that's called hibernating.

Other animals like the cold.

Some birds stay in the garden.

Others fly away to warmer places.

Some countries are very hot.

Others are always cold.

Some animals live only where it's hot.

Here are some of those animals.
Do you know their names?

SPRING is the time for...

lambs and chicks,

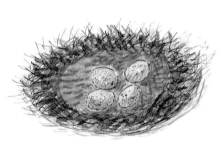

eggs in nests,

sudden showers,

buds on trees.

SUMMER is the time for...

butterflies floating,

flowers growing,

long lazy picnics

and holidays by the sea.

AUTUMN is the time for...

falling leaves,

fruit on trees,

harvest time,

bonfires,

berries, nuts and squirrels.

WINTER is the time for...

skating, sledging

and snowball fights.

Bare branches,

gloves and scarves,

whistling winds and glowing fires.

People say funny things about the weather.

Rain rain go away, come again another day.

Red sky at night, shepherds' delight.
Red sky in the morning, shepherds' warning.

If the cows are lying down
it's going to rain.

The north wind doth blow
and we shall have snow.

Do you know any weather rhymes?

If the sun shines when it's been raining, sometimes you can see a rainbow in the sky.

What do you do on a WET day?

It's fun to watch the weather change,
but what happens if there's too much...

rain,

sun,

wind

or snow?

Whatever the weather is like,

it gets dark at the end of each day.

Night animals go hunting.

The moon and stars light up the sky.

What will the weather be like tomorrow?

First published in Great Britain 1995
by William Heinemann Ltd
Published in paperback by Mammoth 1996
an imprint of Reed International Books Ltd
Michelin House, 81 Fulham Road, London SW3 6RB
and Auckland, Melborne, Singapore and Toronto

Copyright © Catherine and Laurence Anholt 1995
All rights reserved
ISBN 0 7497 2291 6

A CIP catalogue record for this title
is available from the British Library

Produced by Mandarin Offset Ltd
Printed and bound in Hong Kong